One Hundred Famous Haiku

One Hundred Famous
HAIKU

Selected and Translated into English by
Daniel C. Buchanan, Ph. D.

JAPAN PUBLICATIONS, INC.
Tokyo and San Francisco

To my children—
George, Daniel Jr., Katharine, and Margaret-Anne

Japan Publications, Inc.
Japan Publications Trading Company
200 Clearbrook Road, Elmsford, N.Y. 10523, U.S.A.
1255 Howard St., San Francisco, Calif. 94103, U.S.A.
P.O. Box 5030 Tokyo International, Tokyo 101–31, Japan

ISBN 0–87040–222–6
LCC Card No. 72–95667

First printing: May 1973
Second printing: December 1973
Third printing: July 1975
Fourth printing: October 1976
Printed in Japan by Kenkyusha Printing Co.
Design and typography by Norio Okawa

Contents

Acknowledgments

Many Japanese friends, too numerous to name, early interested me in haiku. Japanese literature is full of these seventeen-syllable gems of thought, which are freely quoted by writers, playwrights, speech-makers, and the general public. About fifteen years ago, I began to collect some and to try my hand at translating them. I showed several to Mr. Andrew Y. Kuroda, Chief of the Japanese Section, Orientalia Division of the Library of Congress. He encouraged me to make translations of more haiku and to have them published in book form. I am greatly indebted to Mr. Kuroda for valuable suggestions and help in finding a publisher for this little volume. I also wish to thank Professor Wayne Shumaker of the University of California in Berkeley for carefully reading my manuscript and suggesting helpful changes in wording. To my wife, Margaret W. Buchanan, go my grateful thanks for constant encouragement. Not only has she read my manuscript many times, but she has also given me valuable ideas for making this little book readable and attractive.

Preface

Hundreds of years ago as the result of poetry contests there evolved in Japan a form of verse known as *hokku*, "sending verse," or *haiku* "play verse." Such verses were also called *haikai* "suitable play," but the word haiku is now in more general use. The form is very simple—only three lines, five syllables in the first line, seven in the second, and five in the third, a total of seventeen syllables. Within this limited compass a great variety of thought may be expressed. Some of the favorite subjects of the Japanese muse are the brevity of life, women, birds and other animals, insects, trees and flowers, mountains, the moon, sunrise, snow, rain, mists, and other aspects of nature. There is always a seasonal reference, sometimes very indirect, as "a cold moon"—winter, "plum blossoms"—spring, "fireflies"—summer, or "maple leaves"—autumn.

In haiku there is much use of symbolism, and the hidden suggestion is often subtle, though expressed in simple language. Keen observation and love of nature are shown. These outstanding characteristics of Japanese poetry are frequently accompanied by considerable appeal to emotion. Many haiku are beautiful word pictures, but not elaborate description. There is much understatement and omission, the reader being left to fill in the idea and make his own interpretation. Not a few haiku may be interpreted in a number of different ways, the Japanese language being very flexible. Puns are highly valued in both speech and writing.

The strong influence of Zen Buddhism with its emphasis on mysticism and contemplation is evident in many of the verses. This is not surprising since many haiku writers were itinerant priests or members of monasteries.

Haiku are meant to be read over and over again, for often with each reading a new interpretation may be gained. Since each Japanese word ends with one of the five vowel sounds a, i, u, e, o, or the consonant n; the voice reading of haiku can be beautiful and most pleasing, some of the lines being definitely onomatopoeic. The reader, however, will look in vain for such characteristics of occidental poetry as rhyme, rhythm, or special accentuation.

For the benefit of those who know some Japanese but cannot read Chinese ideographs *(kanji)* or Japanese syllabary *(kana)*, each haiku is printed in *romaji*, the Romanized form of the original Japanese. In making the translations I have endeavored to follow in English the haiku form of three lines with a total of seventeen syllables. Scholars will be pleased to see the poems printed in the original Japanese script. The explanatory notes, while a work of supererogation for some readers, may prove interesting and helpful to the majority.

Notes to the Reader

Japanese is a comparatively easy language to pronounce since every word ends in a vowel or the consonant n. Vowels are pronounced as follows:

> a like a in *father,* but slightly shorter.
> e like e in *pen.*
> i like i in *machine,* but slightly shorter.
> o like the final o in *tobacco.*
> ō like o in *over.*
> u like u in *unite,* but slightly shorter
> ū like u in rude.

Consonants are pronounced as in English, except r which has a slight d sound. There is no l consonant. Each consonant is pronounced separately but rapidly even when they come together. Combinations of vowels are also pronounced separately. Accentuation is so hard to distinguish that the beginner in Japanese should endeavor to give the same emphasis to each syllable.

Spring

Haru

Ume-ga-ka ni
Notto hi no deru
Yamaji kana.
　　　—Bashō

On sweet plum blossoms
The sun rises suddenly.
Look, a mountain path!

梅が香に
のっと日の出る
山路かな

The combination of the beauty and fragrance of plum blossoms lining the mountain path as the sun appears over the horizon, excites the wonder and admiration of the poet.

Matsuo Bashō (1644–1694), the greatest haiku writer of all time, was born in a poor but samurai family in southern Japan. When quite young he became the page and friend of Sengin, son of a nobleman, the Lord of Iga Province. Twelve years later, on the death of Sengin, Bashō entered the monastery on Mount Kōya. He did not stay there very long but proceeded to Kyoto, the capital of the empire, where he studied haiku under Kigin, and shortly afterwards started his own school. Talented men became his pupils, quite a number of whom established their own schools of haiku.

Haru nare ya!
　Namo naki yama no
　　Usu-gasumi.
　　　　　　—Bashō

Has spring come indeed?
On that nameless mountain lie
Thin layers of mist.

春なれや
名もなき山の
薄霞

"Nameless," not because the mountain had no name, but because the poet did not wish to single out one from the many beautiful peaks in the Nara region. Note how Bashō contrasts the beginning of the season with the beginning of the day. Mist-layered mountains are commonly seen in Japan and would not be considered remarkable by the ordinary person, but the poet sees and hails them for their intrinsic beauty and as harbingers of the vernal season.

Shihō yori
    Hana fuki irete
        Niō-no-umi.

                    —Bashō

From all directions
Cherry blossoms blow upon
Two-Deva-Kings-Lake.

四方より
花吹き入れて
鳰（仁王）の海

This lake, better known as Lake Biwa or Ōmi Lake, is the largest fresh water body in Japan; the thousands of cherry trees growing on its shores are a marvelously beautiful sight when they are in full flower. The Two Deva Kings (*niō*), Indra and Brahma, are important Hindu deities whose enormous statues are often to be found to the right and left of the gates of Buddhist temples, to guard them against demons.

Kane kiete
  Hana no ka wa tsuku
    Yūbe kana.
            —Bashō

Temple bells die out.
The fragrant blossoms remain.
A perfect evening!

鐘_{かね}きえて
花_{はな}の香_かはつく
夕_{ゆう}べかな

Note how marvelously the poet in seventeen syllables has caught the beauty and serenity of a late spring evening at a mountain temple. One can almost hear the deep toll of the huge bell, see the white and pink blossoms of the cherry trees, and smell their delicate fragrance. In Japanese literature, whenever blossoms or flowers are mentioned, with no others designation, the reader is given to understand that cherry blossoms are meant. At the close of day in rural areas temple bells often strike the hour.

Fūryū no
　Hajime ya! oku no
　　Ta-ue uta.
　　　　　　　—Bashō

Pristine elegance!
There, in the interior,
The rice-planting song.

風流の
初めや奥の
田植え歌

One day Bashō and a friend were having a discussion as to whether elegance could be found in rural areas. While they were debating the point, a beautiful song came from an adjoining field where women were transplanting rice. Whereupon Bashō composed this haiku, thus indicating that elegance or refinement, so widely regarded in the big city of Edo, actually had its beginning in the rice-planting songs.

Kome no naki
  Toki wa hisago ni
    Ominaeshi.
              —Bashō

At a riceless time,
The gourd receptacle holds
An *ominaeshi*.

米こめ の な き
時とき は 瓢ひさご に
女おみなえし郎花

"Riceless times" for peasants and the poor were frequent in seventeenth-century Japan. People then would eat barley, sweet potatoes, or weeds from the field. The *ominaeshi*, a flower known for its fragile beauty, is not inedible. The Chinese ideographs for it can also be read *musume no hana*, which translated into English is "maiden flower." Bashō, a priest, was very poor and depended on his friends and disciples for food. A receptacle made from a gourd was kept outside his dwelling into which rice and other articles of food were put by the poet's admirers.

Ochizama ni
Mizu koboshi keri
Hana tsubaki.
　　　—Bashō

Falling upon earth,
Pure water spills from the cup
Of the camellia.

落_お
ち
ざ
ま
に

水_{みづ}
こ
ぽ
し
け
り

花_{はな}
椿_{つばき}

In Japanese literature the samurai is often compared to the camel-
lia whose flower lasts only a few days and then falls in one piece
to the ground. So like that of the flower, the samurai's life may
be brilliant but short. In this poem we see an indirect reference to
the Zen philosophical teaching on the shortness and uncertainty
of life.

Yase sune mo
  Areba zo, hana no
  Yoshino-yama.
        —Bashō

Though my shanks are thin
I go where flowers blossom,
Yoshino Mountain.

痩やせすねも
あればぞ花はなの
吉よし野のやま山

So beautiful and numerous are the wild cherry blossoms of Mount
Yoshino in Nara Prefecture that they are well worth the six-
thousand-foot climb by an old man whose legs are thin and less
strong than they were in youth. So the good life is a long and
upward climb, especially arduous in the latter years; but the final
reward is satisfaction.

Sakura chiru
Nawashiro-mizu ya
Hoshi-zuki-yo.
— Buson

Cherry blossoms fall
On watery rice-plant beds:
Stars in the moonlight.

桜
ちる
苗
代
水
や

さくら
なわ
しろ
みづ

星
月
夜

ほし
づき
よ

Equally famous as a painter and a poet, Taniguchi Buson (1716–1783) has painted here an exquisite word picture. The fallen cherry blossoms on the water of rice-plant beds are likened by the poet to the stars studding the sky of a bright moonlit night.

雨^{あめ}の日^ひや
都^{みやこ}に遠^{とお}き
桃^{もも}のやど

Ame no hi ya!
　　Miyako ni tōki
　　　　Momo no yado.
　　　　　　　　—Buson

The day is rainy.
Far from the capital is
My peach-blossom home.

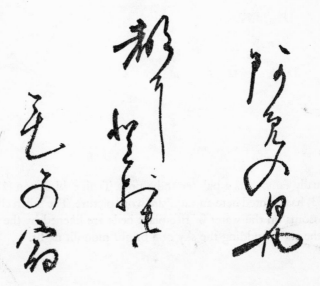

Though he is living in the capital (Kyoto), because of the rainy day, the poet has nostalgic longings for his rural home with flowering peach trees around it.

Haru no umi
Hinemosu notari,
Notari kana.
—Buson

The sea at springtime.
All day it rises and falls,
Yes, rises and falls.

春<ruby>海<rt>はる</rt></ruby>
の
<ruby>海<rt>うみ</rt></ruby>
ひ ね も す の た り
の た り か な

The sea at spring, though generally undisturbed by storms, none-theless moves continuously. So, too, in the life of a person or a nation there are always ups and downs and a certain amount of monotony. As you read this poem aloud, do you catch the rise and fall of the waves in the onomatopoeic *notari, notari?*

Kinō ini,
　Kyō ini, kari no
　　Naki yo kana.
　　　　　　　—Buson

Going yesterday,
To-day, to-night . . . the wild
　geese
Have all gone, honking.

昨き
日の
に

今きょ
日う
に
雁かり
の

な
き
夜よ
か
な

All lovers of wild life can share the grief of the poet as he laments the departure of the wild geese for their nesting grounds. One might ask where is the seasonal reference in this haiku. To the Japanese mind, the flight of the wild geese from their winter home is a clear reference to spring.

Teshoku shite
 Niwa fumu hito ya
  Haru oshimu.
          —Buson

Candlestick in hand,
 See, he strolls through the
   garden,
Grieving over spring.

手<ruby>燭<rt>しょく</rt></ruby>して
庭<ruby>に<rt></rt></ruby>ふむ<ruby>人<rt>ひと</rt></ruby>や
<ruby>春<rt>はる</rt></ruby><ruby>惜<rt>お</rt></ruby>しむ

The last Japanese word in this haiku *oshimu*, here translated "grieving," has the additional meaning of "reluctant." Hence, the man who strolls, candlestick in hand, through his garden is grieving over the departure of spring and reluctant to let the season go.

Haru kaze ni
　Osaruru bijo no
　　Ikari kana!
　　　　　—Gyōtai

By the spring breezes
The beautiful girl is pushed.
What indignity!

春^{はる}
風^{かぜ}に
おさるる美^び女^{じょ}の
いかりかな

Gyōtai (1732–1792) notices the displeasure of the lovely young woman when the spring breeze disarranges her hair and clothing. While interested in the scene, he is also amused at the reaction of the girl.

美うつく しき
凧たこ あがりけり
乞食こじき 小屋こや

Utsukushiki
　　Tako agari keri
　　　　Kojiki-goya.
　　　　　　　　—Issa

How beautifully
That kite soars up to the sky
From the beggar's hut.

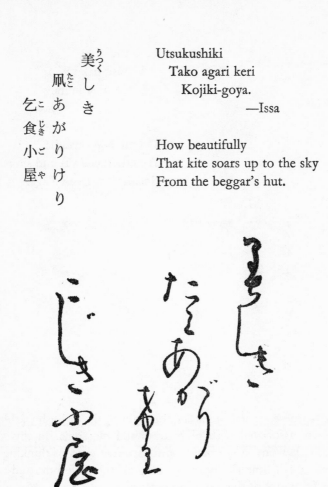

Issa (1763–1827), a poor man himself, was pleased to see the beautiful flight of a kite from a lowly hovel, expressive of the hidden desires and ambitions of its occupant.

Kuwa no e ni
Uguisu naku ya
Ko-ume mura.
　　　　—Issa

On the hoe's handle
A nightingale sits and sings.
Small-plum-tree village.

鍬くわの柄え に
鶯うぐいす なく や
小こ梅うめ村むら

In Japanese art and literature, the nightingale (or bush warbler) is always associated with plum trees and blossoms. In this short poem, persons in sympathy with Japanese ways of thinking and feeling can hear the beautiful song of the little bird and smell the fragrance of the plum blossoms.

Harusame ya!
　　Nezumi no nameru
　　　Sumida-gawa.
　　　　　　—Issa

A gentle spring rain.
Look, a rat is lapping
Sumida River.

春雨や
鼠のなめる
隅田川

Note how the gentle drizzle is balanced with the lapping of the rat. In this poem you can almost hear the drip, drip, drip of the gentle spring rain and the lap, lap, lap of the thirsty little rodent. With plenty of good drinking water all around him why should the rat go to the big Sumida River? Force of habit? So we humans often habitually go to much trouble and do unnecessary things.

(Hato ikenshite iwaku)
Fukurō yo,
   Tsurakuse naose
     Haru no ame.
         —Issa

(The dove's advice)
" Come on now, friend owl,
Change your facial expression.
This is the spring rain."

（鳩意見していわく）
梟よ
面癖なおせ
春の雨

A keen observer of animals and birds, Issa noticed that doves do not mind the rain but owls generally remain in holes in trees and rocks during wet weather. He humorously puts into the mouth of the dove good advice to owls—and to humans as well—not to be worried and frustrated by conditions and events over which they have no control. Issa is noted for his warm, friendly good humor and his love for birds and beasts. The first line is introductory. The haiku actually starts with *Fukurō yo* ("Come on now, friend owl").

Yuki tokete,
　Mura ippai no
　　Kodomo kana.
　　　　　—Issa

Snow having melted,
The whole village is brimful
Of happy children.

雪とけて
村いっぱいの
子供かな

With the snow melted and the arrival of warm weather, the children can again play happily in the village street, and the poet participates in their simple joy. Issa greatly loved children. He himself had five, but they all died young.

あっさりと
春は来にけり
浅黄空

Assari to
　Haru wa ki ni keri
　　Asagi-zora.
　　　　　　　—Issa

Pure simplicity
Marks the arrival of spring—
A pale yellow sky.

Issa was a simple man of quiet tastes who greatly enjoyed the "pure simplicity" of early spring, for more often than not this is the way the vernal season would arrive. So too, important changes take place in life, often quietly and with little show.

Kano momo ga
Nagare-kuru ka yo
Haru-gasumi.

—Issa

Will that very peach
Come floating down the small
    stream?
The mists of springtime.

かの桃が
流れくるかよ
春霞

The reference is to the fairy tale of *Momotarō* (Peach-boy), who was found in a large peach that floated towards an old woman as she was washing clothes by a stream near her hut. On seeing a picture of an old woman at a stream washing her clothes, Issa recalled the tale of the peach-boy and wondered whether a peach would come floating by.

Kado kado no
Geta no doro yori
Haru tachinu.
— Issa

At every doorway,
From the mud on wooden clogs,
Spring begins anew.

門々の
下駄の泥より
春立ちぬ

The very mud on the clogs is a sign of spring, for in winter the ground is too hard to adhere to the clogs. Issa rejoices in muddy footgear as a sign that spring has again come to bless man. Thus what is generally regarded as ugly and undesirable may often be a harbinger of beauty and joy, but it requires a poet to see it.

Suzume-go ya!
Akari shōji no
Sasa no kage.
　　　　—Kikaku

See the young sparrows!
On paper-thin sliding doors,
Bamboo-grass shadows.

雀子や
あかり障子の
笹の影

In Japanese literature and pictorial art, sparrows and bamboo-grass are often associated. It is a beautiful spring day. The sun shines on clumps of bamboo grass in the garden casting brocade-like shadows on the pure white, translucent paper panels of the home's sliding doors. Outside young sparrows are flitting about and chattering happily. Such a scene probably inspired the poet to compose the above haiku. Kikaku (1661–1707) was one of the ten special pupils of Bashō.

Hi wa ochite
　　Masu ka to zo miyuru
　　Haru no mizu.
　　　　　　—Kitō

The sun having set,
Has it increased in volume
The waters of spring?

日
は
落
ち
て

増
す
か
と
ぞ
み
ゆ
る

春
の
水

Kitō (1741–1789) seems to feel that after the sun has set and with nothing left to distract one's attention, the volume of water from the gentle spring rain appears to increase. Plenty of rain is most desirable in spring to soften the soil of the paddy fields and prepare them for planting rice, the principal crop of the farmer.

Na no tsukanu
    Tokoro kawayushi,
      Yama-zakura.
                —Goshun

In unamed, remote
Places, charming and lovely,
Wild-cherry blossoms!

名な　の　つ　か　ぬ
所ところ　か　わ　ゆ　し
山やま　ざ　く　ら

In spring natural beauty may be found everywhere, even among remote and nameless mountains. With seeing eyes and appreciative minds, we too may discover beauty and satisfaction even in some of the most secluded and unlikely places. Goshun, also known as Gekkei, was born in 1752 and died in 1811.

地に<ruby>地<rt>ち</rt></ruby>におりて
<ruby>凧<rt>た</rt></ruby>にたましい
なかりけり

Chi ni orite
　Tako ni tamashii
　　Nakari keri.
　　　　　—Kubonta

Since settling to earth
The high spirit of that kite
Has gone completely.

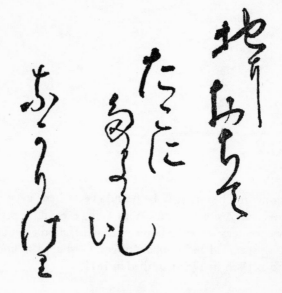

Men when soaring in the heady air of success have plenty of spirit but often lose it if forced to come to earth and do the humdrum things of life. Kubonta was born in 1881 and died in 1924.

Haru-kaze ya!
   Mugi no naka yuku
      Mizu no oto.
            —Mokudō

A gentle spring breeze!
Through green barley plants rushes
The sound of water.

春^{はる}風^{かぜ}や
麦^{むぎ}の中^{なか}ゆく
水^{みず}のおと

Mokudō (1665–1723), a samurai of the Hikone clan, was a pupil of Bashō. As the spring breezes pass over them, the waving young barley plants make a swishing sound like running water and, at a distance, often resemble the green waves of a bay or lake.

Rakka eda ni
Kaeru to mireba
Kochō kana.
　　　—Moritake

A fallen blossom
Is coming back to the branch.
Look, a butterfly!

落花枝に
かへると見れば
胡蝶かな

Moritake (1473–1549) was a high-ranking Shinto priest of the Ise Shrine and one of the earliest writers of haiku. What a simple but beautiful word picture he has painted!

Hatsu-kochi no
Kawaya no akari
Ugoki keri.
　　　　　　—Ōemaru

The first east wind makes
The light in that old privy
Flutter and flicker.

初東風の
厠のあかり
うごきけり

Ōemaru (1719–1805) was a businessman and a pupil of the poet
Ryōta. Even such a lowly thing as the flicker of the light in an
outdoor toilet is noticed by the nature-loving poet, and the breeze
that causes it is hailed as the forerunner of spring.

Haru no hi ya!
  Niwa ni suzume no
    Suna abite.
                —Onitsura

A lovely spring day—
Out in the garden sparrows
Are bathing in sand.

春は の 日ひ や
庭にわ に す ず め の
砂すな あ び て

Onitsura (1661–1738) was a monk and pupil of Bashō. Watching sparrows taking sand baths, the poet is led to reflect on the beauty of the spring day. We, too, if our hearts are attune to nature and to the great Creator of all, can find much enjoyment in the simple things of life.

Uguisu ya!
  Ume ni tomaru wa
    Mukashi kara.
          —Onitsura

Look, a nightingale!
They have lighted on plum-trees
From antiquity.

鶯や
梅にとまるは
昔から

In Japanese literature and art, the nightingale (or bush warbler) is always linked with plum-trees. The tree is the first to flower in early spring and frequently blooms while snow is still on the ground. Hence, it is admired by the Japanese as a brave tree.

曙や　麦の葉末の　春の霜

Akebono ya!
　Mugi no hazue no
　　Haru no shimo.
　　　　　—Onitsura

A new day has dawned!
On the tips of barley plants
The frost of springtime.

Sunrise turning the frost on the tips of green barley plants into sparkling emeralds. What a beautiful word picture the poet monk has painted for us!

Gaikotsu no
　Ue wo yosōte
　　Hana-mi kana.
　　　　　—Onitsura

Skeletons dressed up
In gala attire are out
For flower viewing.

骸骨の
上をよそうて
花見かな

Instead of admiring the charming scene of beautifully dressed
people picnicking under trees laden with lovely cherry blossoms,
the old monk cynically reflects on the shortness of life—a natural
reaction for a priest of Zen.

Umazume no
 Hina kashizuku zo
  Aware naru!
          —Ransetsu

The barren woman
Is attending the little dolls.
So pitiable!

石女の
ひなかしづくぞ
哀れなる

Ransetsu (1654–1707) looks with pity on the barren woman (literally "stone woman") as she arranges on shelves the figurines for Doll Festival Day (*Hina Matsuri*). That day, celebrated on March 3, is a special holiday for girls all over Japan; May 5 is Boys Day. In recent times both festivals have been joined and are celebrated on May 5, a national holiday known as Children's Day (*Kodomo no Hi*).

Furi-aguru
　　Kuwa no hikari ya!
　　　Haru no nora.
　　　　　　—Sanpū

Up-swinging mattocks
Glittering in the sunshine!
Spring is in the fields.

振り上ぐる
鍬のひかりや
春ののら

The gleaming mattocks of the peasants breaking the ground pre-
paratory to spring planting remind the poet that the vernal season
has arrived. Sanpū (1647–1732) was one of the ten special pupils
of Bashō.

Hina no kao
Ware zehi naku mo
Oi ni keri.
　　　　　—Seifu

The faces of dolls.
In unavoidable ways
I must have grown old.

雛の
かお
我ぜひなくも
老いにけり

Seifu (1650–1721) was a poetess nun. As she views the dolls arranged on the shelves for Doll Festival Day (March 3rd) and realizes that they no longer seem to interest her, she reflects that she is unavoidably getting on in years—a hint of Buddhist fatalism.

Shima-jima ni
　Hi wo tomoshi keri
　　Haru no umi.
　　　　　—Shiki

On all the islands
Glittering lights now appear.
The sea at springtime.

島々に
灯をともしけり
春の海

The lights from neighboring islands and fishing boats in the bay combine to make a most beautiful night picture of a calm sea in early springtime. As a boy in Takamatsu, about the time that Shiki (1867–1902) died, I frequently saw just such scenes from my bedroom window facing the Inland Sea.

Haru no hi ya
Hito nani mo senu
Komura kana.
　　　　—Shiki

A sunny spring day,
People are doing nothing
In the small village.

春は
人ひと
小こ
村むら
か
な

の
何なに
も
せ
ぬ

日ひ
や

The poet was delighted to note that, busy as the villagers usually
are, sometimes they can fully relax on a spring day and just enjoy
doing nothing. We in our tense, modern world would do well
to learn that lesson.

菅笠を
着て
かがみ見る
茶摘みかな

Suge-gasa wo
Kite kagami miru
Chatsumi kana.
—Shikō

Wearing her sedge-hat
She preens before the mirror,
A tea-leaf picker.

Even a peasant tea-leaf picker is a woman, always careful of her appearance and mindful of her attractiveness. Shikō (1665–1731) was first a Buddhist priest but later became a physician.

Kore wa kore wa
　　To bakari, hana no
　　　　Yoshino-yama.
　　　　　　　　—Teishitsu

My, oh my! No more
Could I say; viewing flowers
On Mount Yoshino.

これはこれは
とばかり花の
吉し野のやま山

In April the hills of Mount Yoshino are white with wild cherry trees in bloom, and thousands of people go up from the cities to enjoy the glorious sight. The beauty was so overwhelming that no words could adequately describe it for the poet Teishitsu (1610–1673).

Mugi kuishi,
　　Kari to omoedo
　　　Wakare kana!
　　　　　　—Yasui

Barley they do eat,
The wild geese that I yearn for:
But when they depart. . . .

麦<ruby>麦<rt>むぎ</rt></ruby>
雁<ruby>雁<rt>かり</rt></ruby>
別<ruby>別<rt>わか</rt></ruby>れ

麦<ruby>むぎ</ruby>く
雁<ruby>かり</ruby>い
と し
別<ruby>わか</ruby>お
れ も
か え
な ど

In a land where food was scarce, the barley eaten by wild geese could not well be spared, yet the poet reflects that when the beautiful birds leave (for their nesting place). . . . The reader is expected to understand and express for himself the resultant sorrow and lonesomeness. Yasui (1657–1743) was a merchant of Nagoya and one of Bashō's pupils.

The second line of this haiku "Kari to omoedo" can also be translated,

　　　"I'm thinking of the wild geese"

Sake nakute
    Nan no onore ga
        Sakura kana.
                    —Anonymous

Without flowing wine
What good to me are lovely
Cherry trees in bloom?

酒{さけ}なくて
何{なん}の己{おのれ}が
桜{さくら}かな

A freer translation:

        Without wine, even
        Beautiful cherry blossoms
        Have small attraction.

In April, when cherry trees are in bloom in Japan, whole families, groups of friends, or business associates take the day off and go to some noted beauty spot to picnic together. They can frequently be seen accompanied by geisha or other female companions, dancing or seated or lying under the blossom-laden branches, eating, drinking, singing, and having an uproariously good time. Great quantities of sake are consumed, and many get so drunk they can barely stagger home in the evening. Hence, the above popular haiku.

Summer

Natsu

Hototogisu
　　Naki, naki tobu zo
　　　Isogawashi.
　　　　　　　—Bashō

Hark to that cuckoo,
Ceaselessly singing in flight,
How very busy!

郭公
鳴きなき飛とぶぞ
いそがわし

A beautiful word picture which also teaches humans to keep oc-
cupied and to be joyful in work. The second line of the Japanese
poem can be translated literally, "Singing, singing while flying."

Natsu-kusa ya!
　Tsuwamono-domo ga
　　Yume no ato.
　　　　　—Bashō

You summer grasses!
Glorious dreams of great war-
　　riors
Now only ruins.

夏草<ruby>夏<rt>なつ</rt></ruby><ruby>草<rt>くさ</rt></ruby>や
つわものどもが
<ruby>夢<rt>ゆめ</rt></ruby>のあと

This poem was composed as Bashō sat and wept over the grass-covered remains of Takadate Castle, the headquarters of the great Fujiwara clan. The glories of yesterday too soon are forgotten and become the ashes or weed-covered remains of today.

Ie wa mina
  Tsue ni shiraga no
  Haka mairi.
              —Bashō

All the family
Equipped with staves and grey-
  haired,
Visiting the graves.

家は皆
杖に白髪の
墓詣り

Summer is the season for visiting the graves of ancestors. On this occasion, the poet, noticing that all in the family group are quite elderly, implies that before long they, too, will be laid to rest.

Kasa mo naki
  Ware wo shigururu ka
    Nanto nanto!
        —Bashō

With no bamboo hat
Does the drizzle fall on me?
What care I of that?

笠かさもなき
我われをしぐるるか
なんとなんと

The last line of this haiku might also be freely and colloquially rendered, "I don't give a darn." Note that in the original Japanese of this haiku there are eight syllables in the second line and six in the third line, a total of nineteen syllables for the whole poem, instead of the usual seventeen. Great masters sometimes depart from hard and fast rules.

The poet's indifference to rain is a lesson to others to accept unpleasant conditions and experiences philosophically. Too many people let the weather influence their attitudes and actions towards others.

Samidare wo
Atsumete hayashi
Mogami-gawa.
　　　　—Bashō

Early summer rains
Gathering, form the rapid
Mogami River.

五月雨を
集めて早し
最上川

The Japanese word *samidare* translated "early summer rains" is literally "fifth month rain," and since the lunar calendar was in use some three hundred years ago, when Bashō lived, the fifth month was what we now call June, the *nyūbai* or rainy season, when rain often falls incessantly for weeks. It is then that small streams like the Mogami become raging rivers. Two other terms for the "rainy season" are *baiu* and *tsuyu*, both written 梅雨, the Chinese ideographs for "plum-tree rain."

道のべの
木槿はうまに
くわれけり

Michi nobe no
　　Mukuge wa uma ni
　　　　Kuware keri.
　　　　　　　—Bashō

By the roadside grew
A rose of Sharon. My horse
Has just eaten it.

Though a statement of fact, the poem carries overtones emphasized by Zen teachings of the shortness of life, no matter how beautiful.

Yabuiri no
　　Yume ya azuki no
　　　Nieru uchi.
　　　　　　　—Buson

The servant's day off.
Does he dream of that as on
The stove red beans boil?

や　ぶ
夢_{ゆめ}　入_{いり}
煮_に　や　の
え　小_{あずき}
る　豆
う　の
ち

Yabuiri was a semi-annual holiday for apprentices, servants, and other household employees. On January 16 and July 16, these people were permitted to go home for the day, or seek amusement in the city streets, parks, temples, and shrines. On such special occasions red beans (*azuki*) were mixed with rice, boiled, and eaten in the home as a special treat. Dozing by the warm hearth on which his mother had set red beans boiling, what dreams did the young apprentice have? The reader is left to conjecture.

Hata utsu ya
　Michi tou hito no
　　Miezu narinu.
　　　　　　—Buson

The peasant hoes on.
The person who asked the way
Is now out of sight.

畑<ruby>は<rt></rt>た</ruby>うつや
道<ruby>みち</ruby>問<ruby>と</ruby>う人<ruby>ひと</ruby>の
見<ruby>み</ruby>えずなりぬ

Occupied with his own task, the peasant has forgotten the traveling stranger who stopped to inquire the way. So too, we are often so busy with our own duties and work that we pay scant attention to the needs of others.

Tsurigane ni
Tomarite nemuru
Kochō kana!
—Buson

On the temple bell
Something rests in quiet sleep.
Look, a butterfly!

釣り鐘に
止まりてねむる
胡蝶かな

Both a famous poet and a painter, Buson has here given us and generations to come this exquisite picture to enjoy. Note the contrast between the huge, black bell and the delicate little butterfly. This haiku seems to contain Zen overtones of the frailty of life and the imponderableness of fate.

Asagao ni
Tsurube torarete
Morai mizu.
　　　—Chiyojo

The morning-glory
Has captured my well-bucket.
I will beg water.

朝顔に
釣瓶とられて
貰い水

Chiyojo (1703–1775) is generally rated the finest woman haiku writer Japan has produced, and this is probably the most quoted of her poems. It beautifully illustrates the Japanese love for blossoms and nature in general. Rather than break the fragile flower entwining the well-sweep bucket, the peasant girl goes to a neighbor for the needed water.

Tombo-tsuri
　　Kyō wa doko made
　　　Itta yara.
　　　　　　　　—Chiyojo

Dragonfly catcher,
How far have you gone today
In your wandering?

蜻蛉つり
今日はどこまで
行ったやら

This poem was composed after the death of her little son, her only child, who was fond of hunting dragonflies. Though not described directly, the sorrow of the mother is beautifully and poignantly expressed. The third line of the English translation is not in the original Japanese haiku, but it is strongly implied.

Hana sakanu
　Mi wa kurui yoki
　　Yanagi kana.
　　　　　—Chiyojo

Bearing no flowers,
I am free to toss madly
Like the willow tree.

花_{はな}　さ　か　ぬ
身_み　は　く　る　い　よ　き
柳_{やなぎ}　か　な

The poetess states that since she has no " flowers " (her husband and child being dead), she has nothing to attract people and like a willow can be freely tossed about by every wind.

Hirou mono
　　Mina ugoku nari
　　　　Shiohi-gata.
　　　　　　　　—Chiyojo

All things I pick up
Are moving, awash upon
The beach at low tide.

拾^{ひろ}う もの
皆^{みな}うごくなり
潮^{しお}干^ひがた

This verse may be a simple statement of fact, or it may be interpreted: "All things that I obtain on life's strand struggle to leave me." Do we have here a hint of the Buddhist philosophy of despair?

Yase-gaeru
Makeru na, Issa
Kore ni ari.
　　　　—Issa

Oh thin little frog
Don't lose the fight. Issa
Is right here to help.

瘠蛙
負けるな一茶
これにあり

It is said that one day the poet saw a large frog and a little thin one fighting. To encourage the latter he composed the above haiku. Here, Issa shows fellow feeling for the weak. He himself is said to have been a very frail person.

Tsuji-dangi
Chimpunkan mo
Nodoka kana.
　　　　—Issa

A wayside sermon
All nonsense to me, but see
How serene he is!

辻_じ
だ
ん
ぎ

ち
ん
ぷ
ん
か
ん
も

長
閑_{のどか}
か
な

The learned discourse of the itinerant priest impresses the poet far less than the former's serenity. Thus our lives and what we do are often more helpful to others than what we say.

水底を
見てきた顔の
小鴨かな

Minasoko wo
Mite kita kao no
Kogamo kana.
　　　　—Jōsō

" The water bottom
I have seen and come back," says
The face of the teal.

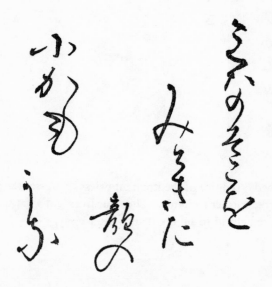

Jōsō (1662–1704) was one of the ten special pupils of Bashō. In this verse the poet seems to indicate that hidden things are often not so interesting as they may first appear to be.

Amagaeru
　Bashō ni norite
　　Soyogi keri.
　　　　—Kikaku

The little rain frog
Rides on a banana tree
As it softly sways.

雨蛙
芭蕉にのりて
そよぎけり

The precarious position of the little green frog on the quivering, swinging and slippery banana tree is a Zen picture of the dangers and uncertainties of life. Note that the Japanese word for banana tree *bashō* is the poetical name of Kikaku's teacher of haiku.

Yūdachi ya !
 Ta wo mimeguri no
  Kami naraba
              —Kikaku

O evening shower,
Make a round of the ricefields
If you are their god.

夕立や
田を見めぐりの
神ならば

This prayer was uttered at Mimeguri, on June 28, 1694, by the poet at the request of farmers when the land had suffered from a long drought. It is recorded that towards evening there came a thunderstorm and a great shower. This haiku contains an interesting play on words, for *mimeguri* is the name of the village where the farmers asked the poet to pray for rain and also has the meaning of " make a round of " or " honorably tour." Hence, the poet is saying, " If you are the god of Mimeguri village, inspect the conditions and see how badly rain is needed."

Yume ni kuru
  Haha wo kaesu ka?
    Hototogisu.
        —Kikaku

In dreams she arrives
My mother. Why send her back?
O heartless cuckoo.

夢に くる
母を かえす か
ほととぎす

The Japanese word for cuckoo *hototogisu* is an onomatopoeia for the bird's call. Since it is heard mostly at night, the bird is supposed to be a messenger from the vale of shadows. While dreaming that his dead mother was with him, the poet is awakened by the call of the cuckoo and chides the bird for sending his beloved parent away. The word " heartless " is not in the Japanese poem though strongly implied.

Chōchō no
　　Shitau hanawa ya
　　　　Kan no ue.
　　　　　　—Meisetsu

Butterflies follow
Lovingly the flower-wreath
Placed on the coffin.

蝶々の
慕うはなわや
棺の上

This haiku was composed at the burial of a dear friend. The Japanese word *shitau* translated " follow lovingly " has also the deeper meaning of " yearn for " or " love dearly." Thus the poet beautifully expresses his yearning for his deceased friend. Meisetsu was born in 1847 and died in 1926.

Asagao ni
　　Kyō wa miyuran
　　　　Waga yo kana.
　　　　　　　　—Moritake

The morning-glory
Today reveals most clearly
My own life cycle.

朝顔に
今日はみゆらん
我世かな

Composed by one of the earliest of Haiku writers, the poem expresses the basic pessimism of Buddhist teaching: that life, however beautiful, is all too fragile and soon comes to naught. This is the poet's *jisei* or " death-bed poem." He was a high-priest of the Ise Shrine.

The morning-glory, or convolvulus, is a symbol of the beauty and briefness of life, since it blooms early in the morning and is withered by noon.

こいこいと
いえどほたるが
とんでゆく

Koi, koi to
　Iedo hotaru ga
　　Tonde yuku.
　　　　　—Onitsura

Come! Come! Though I call
The fireflies are quite heedless
And go flitting by.

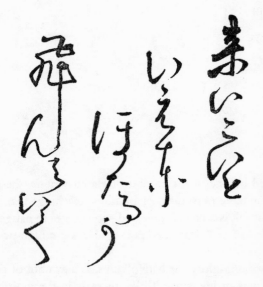

This is said to be Onitsura's first haiku, composed when he was eight. He later developed into a famous poet, entered a Zen monastery, and lived to a great age.

Yūdachi ya!
　　Chie samazama no
　　　　Kaburi-mono.
　　　　　　　　—Otsuyū

An evening shower!
Ingenious wits make use of
Various headgear.

夕立や
智恵さまざまの
かぶりもの

The poet observes that if a sudden shower takes place when peo-
ple are out in the open, they use all sorts of articles to cover their
heads while running for shelter. In the Tokugawa era, when this
haiku was written, the hair arrangements of both men and women
were often quite elaborate. Getting them wet would cause con-
siderable trouble; hence the need to think quickly and provide any
kind of covering for the head. So, too, in life, when unexpected
situations appear, man's wits invent various methods to meet
them. Otsuyū was born in 1675 and died in 1739.

Ta-otome ya!
    Yogorenu mono wa
        Uta bakari.
                —Raizan

You rice-field maidens!
The only things not muddy
Are the songs you sing.

田た
少女おとめや
汚よれぬものは
歌うたばかり

Working at transplanting rice seedlings in a paddy field with mud
up to their knees and much of it splashed on their clothing, arms,
and faces, peasant girls may appear most unattractive. However,
the age-old songs they sing as they plant the seedlings by hand are
so beautiful and charming that they excite the admiration of the
poet. Raizan was born in 1654 and died in 1716.

Machi naka wo
Ogawa nagaruru
Yanagi kana.
　　　　—Shiki

Through the town's center
A little stream flows, bordered
By weeping willows.

町中を
小川ながるる
柳かな

A word picture of a typical Japanese small town, many of which have a brook running through the middle of the main street. Here women gather to wash their rice and clothes while gossiping; children laugh, cry, and play; and old men sit under the shade of drooping willows to meditate, greet their friends, or make an occasional remark.

A talented writer of both prose and poetry, Masaoka Shiki (1867–1902) died of tuberculosis when he was thirty-five. Though a city man, he greatly loved and admired natural beauty and went to rural and mountain areas as often as possible.

Kumpū ya!
  Senzan no midori
    Tera hitotsu.
          —Shiki

A cool summer breeze!
Midst a thousand green moun-
      tains
A single temple.

薫^{くん}風^{ぷう}や
千^{せん}山^{ざん}のみどり
寺^{てら}一^{ひと}つ

The word *kumpū* translated " summer breeze " has also the mean-
ing of " balmy breeze." The literal meaning of the two Chinese
ideographs is " fragrant breeze." One can almost smell the aroma
of the light breeze coming through the pines on a thousand green
mountains and the incense from the altars of the old temple.

Bon-odori
Ato wa matsu-kaze
Mushi no koe.
　　　　—Sogetsu

The all-souls-feast dance!
Afterwards murmuring pines
And insect voices.

盆踊り
あとは松風
虫のこえ

Bon-odori, the All Souls Festival, is observed all over Japan for three days near the middle of July. Family graves are decorated, and food, drink, and often lighted lanterns are placed on them, for it is believed that the spirits of the deceased return to the old family home which is carefully swept and garnished. In the evening at every town and village there is a special folk dance in which old and young of both sexes, wearing their best clothes or newly-starched kimono, participate with great joy and abandon. Late into the night the dancers, clapping their hands, executing fancy steps, and singing the words of an ancient song, circle around a central wooden tower on which a big drum beats out the time. When the dance is over and the participants have returned to their homes, all that can be heard is the swish of the breeze through the pine trees and the chirping of night insects. Sogetsu (1759–1819), a Buddhist nun, has beautifully described the tranquil sounds, pine breezes, and singing insects in the late evening after the noisy and long-lasting dance is over.

Okite mitsu
　　Nete mitsu, kaya no
　　　Hirosa kana.
　　　　　　　—Ukihashi

Sitting up I look,
Lying down I look. How wide
The mosquito net!

起き
寝て
広さ
み
て
か
つ
み
な
　
つ
　
蚊
　
帳
　
の

This verse, attributed to Chiyojo, who is said to have composed it after the death of her husband when she was twenty-seven, was actually written by another woman, the courtesan Ukihashi. Professor Asataro Miyamori, in his *Haiku Poems Ancient and Modern,* states that this haiku appeared in an anthology edited by Deisoku in 1694, a date several years before Chiyojo's birth.

Autumn

Aki

ほとぎす
大竹やぶを
もる月夜

Hototogisu
Ō-takeyabu wo
Moru tsukiyo.
　　　　—Bashō

Hear the sweet cuckoo.
Through the big-bamboo thicket
The full moon filters.

Does the grove of big-bamboo filter the song of the bird, or the moonlight, or both? This haiku like many others may have several meanings. The verb *moru*, generally translated "leak," has the additional meanings of "filter" and "trickle."

Furu-ike ya!
　　Kawazu tobikomu
　　　Mizu no oto.
　　　　　　　—Bashō

Into the old pond
A frog suddenly plunges.
The sound of water.

古池や
蛙とびこむ
水の音

This is perhaps Bashō's best-known haiku. The profound silence in the ancient garden is suddenly broken by "the sound of water," a literal translation of the third line of the poem, as a frog leaps into the pond. During the last ten years of his life, Bashō took up the study of Zen, the contemplative sect of Buddhism. This is clearly reflected in the above haiku.

Mono ieba
Kuchibiru samushi
Aki no kaze.
—Bashō

When a thing is said,
The lips become very cold
Like the autumn wind.

物言えば
唇寒し
秋のかぜ

The philosopher-poet makes the observation that after a thing is said, the lips become quite cold; that is, for the one who made the remark, the situation is as dreary and bleak as the cold autumn wind. The obvious moral—think carefully before you speak.

Aki fukaki
  Tonari wa nani wo
    Suru hito zo.
        —Bashō

It is late autumn
I wonder what my neighbors
Will be doing now.

秋深き
隣は何を
する人ぞ

The harvest has been completed, and the outdoor chores in pre-
paration for winter are done. Since there is stillness in the entire
neighborhood and no further work, the poet wonders what his
industrious farmer friends will do to occupy their time. The self-
forgetting poet is interested in the welfare of his neighbors.

Inazuma ya!
　Yami no kata yuku
　　Goi no koe.
　　　　　—Bashō

A quick lightning flash!
Traveling through the blackness
The night heron calls.

稲妻や
闇のかた ゆく
五位の声

A striking word-picture of an evening storm and a wild bird's reaction. The lightning and the bird both fly through the darkness. The sharp cry of the night heron emphasizes the solitude of the occasion and the suddenness of the storm.

Mono no oto!
　　Hitori taoruru
　　　　Kagashi kana.
　　　　　　　—Bonchō

The sound of something!
All by itself has fallen
That tattered scarecrow.

物の音
ひとり
案山子
かな

のおと
ひとり倒るる
案山子かな

A sudden sound is startling, but when the scarecrow, formerly upright, is found to have fallen, anxious fear is displaced by nervous laughter. Bonchō (?–1714) was one of Bashō's disciples. Though a native of Kanazawa, he was a physician who lived in Kyoto.

Mi ni shimu ya!
　Naki-tsuma no kushi wo
　　Neya ni fumu.
　　　　—Buson

The cold pierces me
As I tramp my dead wife's comb
On our bedroom floor.

身_みにしむや
亡_{なき}妻_{つま}のくしを
閨_{ねや}にふむ

To the coldness of an unheated bedroom in late autumn and the sorrowing coldness in the heart of the man, is added a shiver of apprehension as he steps on the comb, which in Japanese is *kushi*, a word that can also mean "nine deaths." Hence, to avoid misfortune, one should stamp on a fallen comb before picking it up. The first line of the above haiku can also be literally translated, "How it pierces me."*

---

* Daniel C. Buchanan, *Japanese Proverbs and Sayings* (Oklahoma: University of Oklahoma Press, 1964), p. 224.

Mijika yo ya!
　Ashiato asaki
　　Yui-ga-hama.
　　　　　—Buson

How brief is this life!
Faint footprints on the sands of
Yui-ga-hama.

み　じ
足し　か　世ょ
湯ゆ　あ　や
井い　と
が　あ
は　さ
ま　き

The name Yui-ga-hama literally means " Hotspring Beach." In Japan, a volcanic country, there are a number of places where hot water wells up through the sand, but in the town of Kamakura at its southern boundary, there is a beach known as " Yui-ga-hama."

The word *yo* 世 in the first line translated " life," has the meaning of " world " or " era."

The poet Buson's observation on the shortness of life emphasizes extinction or obliteration of personality, a Buddhist teaching. By way of contrast, a hundred years later the American poet Longfellow sang of " footprints on the sands of time " left by great men, which can be a guide and encouragement to all who come afterward.

Shibu karo ka
Shiranedo, kaki no
Hatsu-chigiri.
　　　　—Chiyojo

Whether astringent
I do not know. This is my first
Persimmon picking.

渋かろか
しらねど柿の
初ちぎり

Acclaimed by most Japanese as the greatest haiku poetess of their land, Chiyojo wrote this verse to indicate that she did not know whether her marriage for the first time would be a happy one or not, just as in the picking of a persimmon one cannot tell whether it is astringent or not. The phrase *hatsu-chigiri* has the double meaning of " first picking " or " first engagement."

Tsuki wo mite
   Ware wa kono yo wo
     Kashiku kana.
          —Chiyojo

Having viewed the moon
I say farewell to this world
With heartfelt blessing.

月を見て
我はこの世を
かしくかな

This deathbed ode of the poetess gives expression to the thought that, after viewing one of the most beautiful of all objects—the autumnal full moon—she willingly and with her blessing on the world departs this life. The Japanese word *yo* has the double meaning of " world " and " life."

思うほど
物言わぬ人と
と涼みけり

Omou hodo
　Mono iwanu hito
　　To suzumi keri.
　　　　　—Hyakuchi

With one who muses
But says not a single word
I enjoy the cool.

Companionship is very desirable, but there are times when the beauty and cool of a fall evening are enjoyed more if nothing is said. Fortunate is the person who has a friend who knows when to be silent. Hyakuchi (1749–1836) was one of Buson's pupils.

Oi nureba
　Hi no nagai ni mo
　　Namida kana.
　　　　　—Issa

As I grow older,
Even the much longer days
Bring plentiful tears.

老い
ぬ
れ
ば
日
の
長い
に
も
涙
か
な

This poem conveys the same idea as the familiar Japanese prov-
erb: *Naga-iki sureba haji ōshi*—"A long life has many shames."*
The poet here weeps over the many sorrows and shames he has
experienced and bewails the long days which he pessimistically
predicts will cause him to weep even more.

---

* Buchanan, *Japanese Proverbs and Sayings*, p. 215.

Meigetsu ya!
　　Tatami no ue ni
　　　　Matsu no kage.
　　　　　　　—Kikaku

A brilliant full moon!
On the matting of my floor
Shadows of pines fall.

名月や
たたみの上に
松のかげ

Kikaku was a famous pupil of Bashō. Note the contrast of the black shadows of the pine-tree and the white matting made even whiter by the light of the full moon. The simple beauties of nature and the plain floor covering of the dwelling combine to make a striking picture.

Yū-gasumi
Omoeba hedatsu
Mukashi kana.
                    —Kitō

The mists of evening.
When I think of them, far off
Are days of long ago.

夕^ゆがすみ
思^{おも}えばへだつ
昔^{むかし}かな

Kitō was a pupil of Buson. The evening haze reminds the poet of some of his misty memories of bygone days. The hazy evening is interestingly contrasted with the hazy thoughts of the poet as he reflects on the events of antiquity.

Ki-giku, Shira-giku
Sono hoka no na wa
Naku-mo-gana.
                        —Ransetsu

Gold chrysanthemums!
White chrysanthemums! Others
Need not be mentioned.

黄き
菊ぐ
白し
菊ら
のぎ
ほく
かの
名な
はが

そ
の
ほ
か
の
名な
は

な
く
も
が
な

Ransetsu was a pupil of Bashō. Note that in the Japanese, line one has two extra syllables, making a total of nineteen instead of seventeen.

The sixteen-petal gold chrysanthemum is the crest of the emperor, the symbol of perfection. The pure white chrysanthemum is the emblem of chaste beauty. Hence flowers of other hues are superfluous.

Ashi-ato wo
Kani no ayashimu
Shiohi kana!
—Rohō

Seeing the footprints
The crab becomes suspicious
Look, it is ebb tide!

足跡を
かにのあやしむ
潮干かな

Seeing human footprints on the sand at low tide, the crab wonders where his enemy is and becomes wary. In the ebb tide of his life should not man too walk carefully when he views all the evil and danger around him?

Mi-yashiro ya!
Niwa hi ni tōki
Ukine-dori.

　　　　—Shiki

See the Shinto shrine!
Remote from the garden lights
Floating birds sleep.

御社や
にわ火にとおき
うきね鳥

An exquisite picture of perfect serenity and peace—the dim lights
of the ancient shrine garden and on the outskirts a quiet pond on
which wild waterfowl float, blissfully asleep. Shiki, a talented
writer of both prose and poetry, died of tuberculosis at the age of
thirty-five.

Meisho tomo
Shirade, hata utsu
Otoko kana!
　　　—Shiki

Though a noted place,
The man pays no attention
And keeps on hoeing.

名所とも
知らで畑うつ
男かな

All over Japan there are places especially noted for their beauty or historical interest and given the general designation of *meisho* (famous place). Such noted spots, visited annually by school children and tourists, are often not esteemed by the local peasants. This poem may be simply a comment on the ignorance or the industry of the farmer. It may also be interpreted to mean that people often work so hard that they do not take the time to appreciate their beautiful and interesting environment.

Shira-tsuyu ya!
　　Mufumbetsu naru
　　　　Okidokoro.
　　　　　　　　—Sōin

O white, limpid dew!
With what poor judgement you
　　choose
The place where you lie!

白露や
無分別なる
おき所

Though the dew is addressed, the thoughts of the reader turn to the shortness of lives which appear and vanish on the scenes of time. " Like dew on the ground " is a well-known Buddhist expression. Sōin (1605–1682) was a samurai of the Kumamoto clan.

Ni ri hodo wa
    Tobi mo dete mau
        Shiohi kana.
                —Taigi

For some five miles round
Kites fly and dance in the sky.
It must be ebb tide.

二に　　　　　　　　　　
鳶と　里り
潮しお　も　ほ
干ひ　出で　ど
か　て　は
な　ま
　　う

Taigi (1709–1771) was one of the pupils of Buson. The *ri* was a
unit of measurement 2.44 miles in length, supposedly the distance
the average person could walk in an hour. The birds wheeling
high up in the sky, making a circumference of five miles, remind
the poet of the circular folk dances in rural areas, of which the
Bon-odori (All Souls Festival Dance) is the most widely known.
The last line may be just a description of the scavenger birds
searching for food as they fly over marshy flatlands. It may also
be taken as a reference to the ebb tide of life.

Winter

Fuyu

"Yado kase!" to
Katana nage-dasu
Fubuki kana!
—Buson

"Give lodging tonight,"
He shouts, flinging down his
sword.
See the windblown snow!

宿 か　刀 吹 雪 か な
や せ　かたな ふ ぶき
と と　投 出
な　げ だ
　　　出
　　　す

On entering the inn, the swordsman throws down his weapon to
indicate that he comes with peaceful intent. Was the unknown
man who rushed in from the blizzard (literally "windblown
snow") a fugitive from justice, a half-frozen traveler, or a noble-
man traveling incognito? The reader is left to fill in this startling
picture.

Yuku toshi ya!
  Oya ni shiraga wo
    Kakushi keri.
              —Etsujin

The year is going.
I have kept from my parents
My gray hairs hidden.

行く年や
親にしらがを
隠しけり

In this poem Etsujin (1656–1739?) shows proper filial piety by hiding his gray hair from his aged parents so as not to give them cause for concern. The poet was a well-known disciple of Bashō.

Every Japanese is a year older on New Year's Day, for age is reckoned by the number of years one has seen. Hence, a child born in December becomes two years old on January 1 of the next year.

天も地も
なしただ雪の
降りしきる

Ten mo chi mo
Nashi, tada yuki no
Furi-shikiru.
—Hashin

No sky and no earth
At all. Only the snowflakes
Fall incessantly.

Hashin (1864–?) was a druggist by profession and a native of Kagawa prefecture. His haiku in seventeen syllables is an excellent word picture of a blizzard.

Myōdai ni
Wakamizu abiru
Karasu kana!
　　　　—Issa

As my deputy
It bathes in New Year's water.
See, there is a crow!

名^{みょう}代^{だい}に
若^{わか}水^{みず}あびる
烏^{からす}かな

Observing a crow bathing in a pool of water on New Year's
morning, the poet humorously calls the bird his deputy. Issa is
grateful to the crow for doing what he should have done. In
nearly all of his poems, Issa, a priest, reveals a deep fellow feeling
for birds, frogs, insects, and other creatures in nature. One might
call him the St. Francis of Buddhism.

Arigata ya!
　Fusuma no yuki mo
　　Jōdo kara.
　　　　　—Issa

How very welcome!
Even snowflakes on bedding
Are from the Pure Land.

ありがたや
衾の雪も
浄土から

When Issa died this poem was found under the pillow of his bed.
The Pure Land (*Jōdo*) is the Buddhist paradise. The poet, who was
very poor, lived in a wretched hut. Through cracks in the window
and wall, snow often drifted in and fell on the bedding and floor.
Yet Issa maintained his cheerful spirit.

No mo yama mo
Yuki ni torarete
Nani mo nashi.
　　　　　—Jōsō

Both plains and mountains
Have been captured by the
　　snow—
There is nothing left.

野の
雪ゆき も
に 山やま
に と も
も ら
な れ
し て

Jōsō, one of the ten special students of Bashō, was a follower of
Zen. The nothingness of life, an important teaching of that sect of
Buddhism, is typified by the snow, which has obliterated such
outstandingly distinct natural features as fields and mountains.

Waga yuki to
  Omoeba, karoshi
    Kasa no ue.
          —Kikaku

When I think of it
As my snow, how light it is
On my bamboo hat.

我が雪と
思えば軽し
笠の上

Composed by the poet on seeing a picture of Su Ton P'o, a famous Chinese literary figure, wearing a large hat covered with snow. The general meaning—what is our own never seems burdensome.

Kimi matsu ya
Mata kogarashi no
Ame ni naru.
                    —Shiki

Are you still waiting?
Once more penetrating blasts
Turn into cold rain.

君
ま
つ
や

又
凩
の

雨
に
な
る

What a vivid picture of a friend or lover forgotten and left
waiting! Compare with the poem by Robert Burns, "O Wert
Thou in the Cauld Blast?"

初夢や
秘めてかたらず
一人笑む

Hatsu-yume ya!
　Himete katarazu
　　Hitori emu.
　　　　　　—Shō-u

With the year's first dream
I told no one my secret,
But smiled to myself.

It was believed that the first dream of the New Year, if a good one
and if kept to oneself, would come true. Shō-u was born in 1860
and died in 1943.

E ni kaita
　　Yō na kumo ari,
　　　Hatsu-hinode.
　　　　　　—Shusai

Like a lovely cloud
In a beautiful picture,
New Year's first sunrise!

絵_えに　かいた
よう　なく　も　あり
初_{はっ}日_ひの出_で

Both the rosy cloud and the lovely sunrise on New Year's Day are surpassingly beautiful, but together they make an unforgettable scene.

Index

119